LENT FOR NON-LENT PEOPLE

LENT FOR NON-LENT PEOPLE: "33 THINGS TO GIVE UP FOR LENT" AND OTHER READINGS

JON SWANSON

For Kathryn Anne Swanson
1989-1989

CONTENTS

INTRODUCTION: LENT FOR NON-LENT PEOPLE

This book, this journey, is for people who aren't exactly sure why they are here. We just are. We've heard about Lent, but we aren't Lent people. What we want is a relationship with God, and we are wondering whether "giving up something for Lent" might help.

I understand that struggle. I've been a pastor, a professor, and a social media chaplain. I'm committed to helping people understand following God, whether through my face-to-face work or through my daily blog, 300wordsaday.com, where several of these readings started. But I didn't grow up in a church that celebrated Lent. And I've wrestled with Lent off and on for more than twenty years. (You can read more about the beginning of that process in the appendix.)

The desire to "give up something" for Lent lasts all year. The second most visited post on my blog is one I wrote about Lent in 2011: "33 things to give up for Lent". All year long people come to this post by searching for the topic "give up for

Lent". Which is intriguing, because Lent doesn't last all year. Lent is a name for the time from Ash Wednesday through Easter Sunday. It is forty days (plus six regular Sundays and Easter Sunday).

Lent is an old word that means *spring*. But if you had to pick a phrase that best captures what people think of Lent, it's this: giving up. Not as in *quitting a competition*, but as in *giving up something*. People observing Lent give up something that matters to them. Often it's food, like meat on Friday or sugar for the forty weekdays. Sundays often are free days, exempt from the giving up. As best as I can tell, it started with the idea of helping people appreciate the festivities of Easter. If we spend the time before Easter preparing our hearts and our bodies, the celebration has more significance.

The forty days are designed to resonate with the forty-day seasons that show up in the Bible. Jesus fasted for forty days. Moses was on the mountain for forty days. Noah and his family watched it rain for forty days and forty nights.

Older than the name Lent is the term "fasting". It is also about giving up. Fasting most simply is giving up *that* for *this*. *That* is something good in itself. *This* is something great. *That* is nourishing to a point. *This* is life itself. That's why Lent isn't about giving up sin. Think about it. "I'll give up my affair for forty days. But every Sunday, just for the day, I go back to my mistress." Ludicrous.

It's easy to get legalistic about forty days of fasting. When humans are presented with a boundary, we focus on the boundary. What counts as fasting? How much can you eat without breaking the fast? How long? What health matters? *Focus* may be a better word than Lent, fasting, or giving up. Often, the best way to *give something up* is to choose what to *focus on instead.* In the case of Lent, the intended focus is God. In this book, we'll talk about God a lot.

When I wrote the "33 things" post, I didn't set out to write a title that would get 27,000 views; I just wrote a list of things other than food to give up. But the brief seasonal spike in readers and the steady traffic during the rest of the year intrigues me. I know that people turn to search engines when they want practical spiritual advice. And why not? There is a virtual ton available. But if one of your spiritual goals is following Lent, the challenge isn't in finding what to give up. It's the challenge of actually getting up every day and giving up. And that happens best in relationship, not search.

Search says, "What are all the options?" Relationship says, "How can I live the option I've chosen?" Search is measured in seconds, relationship in lifetimes. Search is the first step. Relationship is the journey.

For example, my friend Tom read the list and said, "So, I can't be last in line anymore?" We laughed, and I explained that I'm challenged by pride, even the pride of always being last, always being the most humble. That exploration of the idea, that conversation with Tom, is relationship.

In ordinary language, this book explores prayer, fasting, and Sabbath. There are eight chapters. You can read them as chapters. But if you look closer, you will find seven sections in each chapter, a reading for every day of Lent and a bonus chapter for the week after Easter. So this can be a daily reader. In each reading, we explore what Lent is, what giving up and committing to can mean. This isn't a book of how to survive a fast. It's not about the health implications, good and bad, of fasting or praying or resting. We're going to give up some time, give some attention, and spend a few minutes, or a few weeks understanding ourselves and God.

Before we go, some introductions. Nancy, who is mentioned here from time to time, is my wife of more than thirty years, and mother of our children. Andrew is married to Allie and Hope is married to Dan. And all of them have been part of my spiritual formation.

For more about Lent and about me, see me five days a week at 300wordsaday.com. Even through Lent.

WEEK 1: PREPARATION AND ASHES

Giving up something for Lent and committing to something for Lent takes preparation. Deciding what to do for Lent can start before Ash Wednesday, the official beginning of Lent. While tradition says, "give up food", there are other things to give up as well. Time, attention, noise, self-gratification—all of these are things we can give up. This chapter gives several ways to start Lent, including 33 things to give up, and then gets us started on the Lenten season.

1. A simple exercise: Blank page

Here's a very simple way to keep Lent:

Take a piece of paper.

Number it from 1-47.

Put it next to your computer or in the bathroom or on the wall next to your bed.

Starting on Ash Wednesday, every day for the next forty-seven, cross off one of the numbers.

When you cross off the last day, it's Easter.

That's it.

That's a Lenten celebration, giving up that moment of time

to make that mark.

And it may be all you can do.

If you want to do more, that's the rest of this book.

2. A simple exercise: Listen to God 7 minutes a day

My friend Matt had an idea. "What if we started talking about 7 x 7 (seven times seven)?" He wasn't talking about forgiveness, which would actually be 70 x 7 (See that story in Matthew 18: 21-35). He wanted to encourage the idea of spending seven minutes every day listening to God, taking about five minutes to read from the Bible and two minutes to pray.

I didn't like the idea at all.

It felt really legalistic. What if you stopped at 6:50 or kept reading until 7:30?

It felt too structured. Listening to God should be about feeling, not formality.

It felt too small. Imagine *scheduling* seven minutes to listen to your spouse?

It felt too cute. What was *magic* about 7 x 7?

And then I started working on my health. I started riding a bike for 25 minutes at a time. That didn't feel legalistic; it was the kind of exercise habit you need to start in order to get stronger. One day Nancy talked about how little we talk on the days that I'm at work all day and all evening. And I realized that there are some days that scheduling seven minutes to listen to her could help us. And then I realized that we *need* simple reminders even in significant relationships.

Many of us have discovered that frequent, brief conversations are as important to building relationship as occasional, long conversations. They build the habit of interaction, the familiarity with tone of voice and manner of speech and style of language.

So I started 7x7 as an enewsletter. It was a daily email with seven minutes worth of reading. It was very helpful for the people who tried it. We're not running the mailing list anymore, but Lent starts this week. One simple practice may be spending seven minutes listening to God.

3. 33 things to give up for Lent

Ash Wednesday is the first day of Lent. Lent is about willingly learning about sacrifice. Lent is about choosing to give up what rightfully belongs to us.

Here are some possibilities of things to give up for Lent:

1. First place in line.
2. The last piece of pie.
3. Second thoughts about commitments.
4. Saying "Just five minutes more" (when they keep you from family).
5. The last word.
6. A fifth. Of something.
7. A quarter-pounder.
8. Forty cents a day. (It adds up to $12 a month and over a year, and with 100 other people, gives a village in

Africa water.)

9. 280 characters (call it "a day without tweeting").

10. Three scowls.

11. A second helping.

12. The last place in line, which demonstrates just how humble we actually are.

13. "Carpool Karaoke" (or whatever kept you from turning off the TV and going to bed last night.

14. Six simultaneous projects.

15. 10 minutes of frantic activity.

16. The Final Four (pool) that consumes your attention for a month.

17. One argument.

18. A fourth pair of shoes.

19. Eating alone.

20. 12 disciples (Jesus did it. At the end. Of course, they left him. So never mind).

21. 8 minutes extra on the snooze.

22. A second glance (at a test, a girl, a guy).

23. The first 15 parking places closest to the door.

24. A five-minute, well-justified rant about the way that person completely mistreated you when they cut you off as you were driving.

25. One minute of worry each hour.

26. 30 minutes that could have been filled with, "Wait, what did I do with that 30 minutes?"

27. Enough loose change to put a stamp on an envelope

with a piece of paper inside that says, "I love you."

28. 60 minutes a week to converse with someone about God (or to read 300 words).

29. Friday. (Or any one day that you spend willingly on the well-being of someone else.)

30. Credit. for number 29.

31. An extra coat.

32. $10,000 (Maybe you could).

33. My will (go with praying "Your will" instead).

4. Ash Wednesday: Deliberate silence

Fasting isn't giving up unhealthy stuff. It is giving up unhealthy dependence on stuff, including noise.

We talk about all the noise that is part of our lives. Not just audible noises, mind you, but the sheer volume of sights and smells and touches and tastes in our lives.

There are constant noises around us, the presence and traces of those we love (and those we don't), the noise of creation, the noise of life. Now add the stream of images and sounds and taste choices of those seeking our attention, those involved in deliberate unsilence.

Lest you wonder whether that last sentence was a criticism of advertisers and marketers and public relaters, I'll remove your doubt.

Yes, it was.

Including me.

I am involved regularly in deliberate unsilence. Every day I generate words and thought images and stories and photos with the intention of disrupting silence. I write 300wordsaday. I tweet. I update Facebook. You generate your own noise, too.

But at 6:30 on Ash Wednesday morning, in a quiet house, I can choose to be silent, or not. I can choose to have noise, or not. I can decide to look at the stream of images and words, or not.

I can decide whether I have an unhealthy dependence on distraction, or not. And that decision to accept silence is the beginning of a fast.

5. Fasting sets a prayer alarm in our hearts

24 hours after giving up coffee, my head starts to ache.

24 hours after giving up Twitter, I get twitchy.

Because 24 hours after giving up anything, the novelty wears off, and our routines click in. A routine is *a set of thoughts and behaviors performed consistently.* We all have them. We all use them. Every day. Fasting disrupts the routine and the routines disrupt fasting. (We'll look at routine more in Chapter Two).

When we are fasting for Lent, we want to blame someone for our crankiness, for our lapses. What seemed so possible on Wednesday morning seems impossible today. We want to blame the devil for tempting us to take a bite of chocolate. We want to blame God who is so hard to please that we have to give up something to make him happy. We blame our spouse for making the coffee that smells so good.

A couple of brief observations. Brief, because on the second day of Lent our concentration isn't very good.

First, don't blame the devil for what you can change yourself. Get the chocolate out of the house.

Second, talk to Jesus about how hard it is.

The point of giving up something for Lent is not to *impress* Jesus. It's pretty hard to impress a part of the team that created everything, the member of that team who died and came back to life. The point of giving up something for Lent is to set a prayer alarm in our souls, a reminder to have a conversation with Jesus, who understands the connection between fasting and prayer from personal experience.

6. Having coffee with Jesus on Friday morning: A prayer

Jesus, I want you sitting here.

I don't want You to be invisible. I don't want to have to be patient. I want the relationship between my friends to be restored. I want that aching, lonely heart to be healed. I want that damaged brain to start working again, just like it was.

I want to know what to say to all my friends.

I want to be able to say, "Jesus loves you and is praying for you and cares more about that person than you ever will." I say it, Jesus, because I know it is true; but, with all due respect, it sounds cliché.

I'd rather have five smooth stones in my hand to fling at the towering Goliath of despair and watch it come crashing down. And still have four in my hand.

I'd rather ... you know what I'd rather have, Jesus? I'd rather have you. Sitting on the deck. By the lake. With a cup of coffee in your hand in the early morning. The two of us looking at the calmness of the lake and you saying,

"See how smooth that is? I made that. And there was the time at another lake and a boat and a storm. And guys, exactly like you, wanted to know that I was awake, that I was paying attention. They yelled at me above the noise of the storm. They thought I didn't care. They thought I was ignoring them. They thought, well, they thought the storm was going to be too much for me. But it wasn't. The storm was easy. It always is. Them trusting me was hard. It always is."

That's what I want. Instead of the ache that I feel right now. I want that coffee and that calm and You.

And what I know is that You do, too.

I mean, *You* want *me*.

(The story of the storm is in Mark 4:35-41.)

7. A Sabbath memoir: Taking off one day in seven

Three decades ago, I taught study skills to college freshmen. I was a logical choice–I had NO such skills when I was a college freshman. I taught about time management (again, a perfect mismatch). I talked about goal-setting and everything else we knew in a pre-David Allen (*Getting Things Done*) era. I also talked about the importance of a Sabbath, one day in seven when we didn't work.

Growing up, Sabbath was always Sunday for my family. We

couldn't work on the yard or cars or anything else like work. We went to church (morning and evening) and then rested or read or spent time with friends.

As I grew older, studying became an important part of my Sundays, especially as I moved into grad school. Or, to be more accurate, the intention to study. Frequently, I didn't get around to the long to-do list, but it filled my Sundays with procrastinator's remorse. I was pretty stressed by the time I was teaching full-time and working on my doctoral dissertation.

Then I realized that fundamental inconsistency in my behavior. I was telling college students about taking a day off, and I wasn't doing it myself. So I quit. On Sundays I wasn't going to do any work related to school: no teaching, no research. I found a tremendous sense of relief. No longer did I feel guilty for procrastinating. The break probably made me more productive. And, I was following something God said that actually made sense.

To be honest, it made sense after I decided. Before that commitment, I would say that a day off was a nice idea, but I just had too much work. After the commitment, I realized that trusting God to know that He made us for six days of work and one day of rest probably was wise. And, as my friend, Steve Jones, says, "Which of the other Ten Commandments are you deciding to break?"

WEEK 2: LENT AS AN EXPERIMENT IN HABIT

Habits are part of our lives. Good ones and bad, habits toward God and toward ourselves. And we can change them. In this first full week of Lent, we'll talk about some of the subtle habits in our lives, things that distract us. Changing these habits - and changing how we look at habit - can result in significant spiritual change.

1. Routine and ritual

I don't think of Lent as a time to form habits. I think of it as a time to give up. But embracing something new always has in it an element of surrender. And surrender always allows something new.

What if we approached Lent as a time of testing? Not *being* tested as much as testing new routines. If I give up ten minutes of web-browsing every morning and spend that ten minutes talking with God, that's a form of fasting. After 40 days, I can find out whether I needed that ten minutes as much as I thought.

In this chapter we're looking at habits. Habits of distraction, affirmation, grazing, activity. Before we get far into Lent, before we look too deeply at those habits, let's talk about routines and rituals.

For me, a routine is *a set of thoughts and behaviors performed consistently*. Repeated actions, routines, shape us and can then remind us of the context. It can be a bad thing, like flashbacks, or it can be a very helpful thing, being reminded of commitments.

It's easy to turn a routine, a way of living, into a ritual. We perform a ritual, hoping it has some value in itself. It's a kind of magic. We wear our lucky underwear. We show up to church every week.

When we look at the Old Testament, we see God, through His prophets, pointing out how actions of sacrifice, fasting, and Sabbath had become rituals to placate God, performed without thinking. Bodies did the sacrifice, minds and hearts were somewhere else. (You can read about this problem in Isaiah 58 and in Malachi.) But just because we ritualize behavior, doesn't mean that we shouldn't look at routine.

Think of it this way: a *ritual* is something we do hoping to influence God. A *routine* is something we do to work on us. A routine, like daily prayer or weekly Sabbath or a season of fasting, can bring our minds back to the story of God's work.

2. Habits of distraction: Using noise to block the silence

Our son, Andrew, was letting me use his car. He didn't need it. He lived in Chicago.

His car had a better stereo than mine. Better meant I could play CDs and use MP3 players. I enjoyed the variety of music, podcasts and news for the first two months I used his car. Then one day I looked in the car and saw an open glove box and a bent CD on the seat. I didn't see the faceplate for the stereo.

I had left the car unlocked, parked in our driveway. Sometime during the day, the faceplate disappeared. And with it my audio traveling companions. What remained were habits.

During the next few weeks, I discovered that I *use* noise like an addict uses drugs. I discovered that when I drive and start talking with God, I finish a couple sentences and reach for the radio. I didn't realize how often I do that until I watched my hand reach for the radio that no longer was there.

What I learned from my silent commute is that I struggle with conversations. Especially conversations with God. I start by saying something. And then, when it's my turn to listen, *I* fill the silence.

Jesus addressed this need for noise, need for talking, with the disciples. As we read in Mark 6, Jesus talked one morning about taking the disciples to a quiet place to get some rest. They had been on an internship. They needed time with him to reconnect. People were all around. So Jesus led them to a quiet place.

When they got to the place, 15,000 of their closest friends showed up, too. But maybe the appearance of a crowd on a quiet day is not as inappropriate as I've always thought. Because all those people showed up, the disciples weren't able to talk privately to Jesus. They had to listen. They had to spend the whole day listening. Sitting. Just part of the crowd. After a season of celebrity, the best thing for them was relative anonymity, listening to Jesus.

Sometimes silence, sometimes anonymity. Listening always requires giving up something.

(The story of feeding the crowd is told in Mark 6:30-44.)

3. Habits of affirmation: The danger of statistics

Most of us snack. At the beginning of 2012, I started working on my health. I had to look at *why* I was snacking. What was happening inside and outside of me that made me think eating something was the appropriate response?

The question became, "When I do *that snacking*, what am I really doing?" That kind of analysis helped me change my snacking. Two years later and forty-five pounds lighter, I've made progress. I'm still learning.

When talking about fasting and Lent, it's too easy to talk about things like weight. So I need to take you to a question I asked during a season of soul-self-examination.

"Why do I look at my blog statistics? When I do that behavior, what am I *really* doing?"

The kind of work I do requires reflection. The words I write have power. They shape how people think, first shaping me, then you. Sometimes the work is scary. I am afraid of where I have to go in my memory, in my soul.

When I start to feel a little stress, a little uncertainty about whether I am doing the right thing, without being aware, I distract myself. I look at one of several online statistics or social media sites. I can say "see, this many hits" or "that person needs an answer from me," and then I feel better and can go on.

But look at that thought process more closely.

I don't want to do the work of writing, because that is personal. The process of writing might reveal things, first to me, then to you, that I don't want to reveal. So, in the space when I could be thinking and wrestling, instead I look at external measures. I think, without thinking, of course, "my value is in what people think of me."

It's a quick fix of reputation crack.

It's a piece of a routine that, left unaltered, will take me in the wrong direction, will keep me grounding my affirmation in you. And I have to be about pleasing God, not you.

It's a routine that I am starting to change. Because I looked closely at one simple question: "When I do that, what am I really doing?"

4. Habits of grazing: Learning Snickers doesn't satisfy

I used to argue strongly on behalf of a Snickers bar as a healthy snack. After all, it has peanuts. That makes it healthier than candy bars like 3 Musketeers which are merely fluffy.

I was helped in the argument by an ad campaign which claimed that if you were looking for satisfaction, Snickers was the place to turn. (I hope that they were suggesting that it was satisfying primarily for those moments when you are hungry.)

What I must acknowledge, however, is that the temporary

satisfaction of the hunger pain comes at a nutritional price. There are other options. There are healthier options. But when there aren't any of the other options around, you go for the Snickers.

What is more satisfying, I am learning, is being able to buy smaller jeans.

What I am also learning is that I wasn't just satisfying my hunger. Often, I eat because I don't want to think. I don't want to sit still and work through the idea or the tough email or the reflective self-examination or the quiet waiting before God.

I think it's why God said to Isaiah,

"Why spend money on what is not bread, and your labor on what does not satisfy? Listen, listen to me, and eat what is good, and your soul will delight in the richest of fair." (Isaiah 55:28)

That hunger that seems to be for a Snickers bar is actually a deeper hunger, a hunger in my soul rather than my stomach. I know full well that we need food. Because we are created with taste buds, I'm pretty sure we are designed to enjoy good food well. I also know that I spend money on snacks that are not good, time on words that don't feed.

But I am slowly shifting my diet of both foods.

5. Habits of mere activity: A question of stopping
Sometimes you just have to stop.

Sometimes you have to stop and listen and ask and listen.

Sometimes you need questions. Simple questions.

Questions of few syllables and deep thought.

When was the last time you stopped?

That's an easy question to ask. That's a very difficult question to be asked. Which is why I am asking us.

In Matthew 11, after denouncing the cities that ignored what He did, Jesus invited people to come and rest. After pointing out that many people had seen miracles and hadn't repented, Jesus called out to weary people.

Apparently, *watching* miracles isn't enough to transform my life. When we ask for miracles, we ought to remember that, I suppose. We think miracles will be so amazing that everyone will be compelled to believe.

But it isn't so.

A miracle observed happens outside us. Repentance happens inside us. With an about-face, we find our lives changed, a turning from the way we were going.

We make much of the turning, of the repenting. Jesus doesn't make much of the turn itself, of the moment of turning. He doesn't say "Stop going there." He says, "Come to me." He speaks of rest, of humility, of burdens being lifted, of gentleness. More than lamenting the lack of repenting, in this text Jesus is encouraging the coming.

Late at night, when being driven by the list, rest seems out of reach. In the morning, when being driven by the list, rest seems long gone. In the middle of the day, between the calls and the visits and the ambiguity and the demands precisely phrased to penetrate our self-restraint, rest seems impossible.

Which is why Jesus offers rest. Someone who has tremendous power and authority likely has the power to calm wind and waves and hearts. How else could it happen? How else could we find rest?

So, then, a question: When *was* the last time you stopped?

6. A tale of tea for Friday

When I don't know what to write, I make tea. When I do know, and I just need to stay awake long enough, I make coffee. Coffee is fuel. But tea is about reflection.

When I make coffee, I scoop the coffee into the coffeemaker. I flip a switch and head to the computer. The coffee brews. I run to the kitchen, fill my cup, and go back to work.

Making tea takes involvement. There are steps along the way. I start the water toward boiling. I listen for the whistle. I choose a cup, pour a bit of hot water in, pour it out. I put the tea bag in. I get the sugar canister, add a bit to the cup, put the canister away. I pour the water into the cup, on top of the tea bag, making sure the water also stirs the sugar in. I bring the cup back to my office and write a bit. Then I take the bag out, put it on the little saucer Hope brought back from Oxford.

There is an attentiveness to making tea that I don't have with coffee, though I like them both.

[pause to remove the tea bag and consider the next part of the metaphor, since you know that's what this must be.]

I want the Bible to give me answers. I want to dump in some

water and some grounds and push a button and get happiness.
A verse a day to a better life. It's almost always more
complicated than that.

It turns out that the best understanding comes when I read a
bit and let it start to simmer. I add a bit of my life to the cup and
pour the hot water in and let it brew.

Tea takes ongoing intention. So does life.

7. The Sabbath isn't about starving

It was Saturday. The disciples were tired and hungry. They
followed Jesus, sleeping wherever, eating whatever. On this
day they were hungry.

They were walking on a path leading through a field. The
grain was ripe. The disciples picked some, rubbed their hands
together so the hulls broke away from the grain. They ate. It
wasn't bread, but it was food. It took the edge off.

"Jesus!"

The voice came from along the path.

"Jesus! Look!"

Jesus looked. A couple of Pharisees, on their short walk to
the synagogue, were pointing: "Your disciples are breaking the
rules of the Sabbath."

The disciples *were* breaking the rules. Picking a few grains
was harvesting. Harvesting was work. Work violated the rest
rules of the Sabbath. The religious people were precisely right.

Jesus responded quickly. He gave them a history lesson. He
pointed out that their heroes broke the Sabbath, too.

It was no surprise, of course, this challenge from the legalistic. Just before this walk through the countryside, Jesus asked people who were tired and weighed down to come and walk with him. These were people who weren't just physically tired. They were tired from living up to expectations. They were tired from having to look over their shoulder, expecting pastors to pester them, expecting Pharisees to flog them. Every step was a burden.

And Jesus says, "Try *my* yoke".

The image is from agriculture. A yoke is a carved wooden bar that fits over the shoulder of an ox. It's what the plow is hooked to, the cart. Built well, it leverages pulling power. Built wrong, it digs in. A yoke is also a way of living, a lifestyle taught by a rabbi, a teacher.

Sometimes the rules don't help with the work. Instead, they cut into the shoulders. But, Jesus says, his way of living gives life. Then He defends hungry disciples eating grain from pointless, pointed rules.

(The story is in Matthew 11:28-12:8.)

WEEK 3: LENT AS A PROPHETIC ACT

Elijah is the most notable of the Old Testament prophets. Near the end of his life, he had a crisis of confidence. It started right after an amazing spiritual success. It ended after a forty-day journey into the wilderness. Elijah's story teaches us that even God's most famous representatives have hard times and sometimes simply need to step out of the chaos long enough to listen to God.

1. The Sunday kind of fear

Last week was a wonderful week. We started down this journey of Lent. You gave up something that mattered. You are getting tiny glimpses of God. And you woke up this morning terrified about the new week.

This morning you realized that some people are feeling threatened by your discipline. It feels like they are out to get you. Most people don't understand what you are doing, particularly if you are with people who don't traditionally acknowledge Lent.

I think we need to talk about prophets.

When God wants to get people's attention, He has lots of options: rainbows, earthquakes, babies. When He wants to explain *why* He's getting their attention, He sends prophets. Prophets speak on God's behalf. As you read through the Bible, they are men and women, old and young, consistent and inconsistent, shepherds, nobles. They have little in common with each other, except this: *God gives them illustrated words.*

They often sound cranky. They speak against the way we routinely live. It's not because they are trying to be contrarian. Quite the opposite. They are speaking the truth, the standard. And everything else is contrary.

Part of their message is always good news: *God's offering this. Stop doing that. Draw near to God. Stop doing what takes you away.* But most of the time, the good news gets ignored. To hear it would mean changing our fundamental orientation to life.

Sometimes prophets are living metaphors. For example, God says to Ezekiel, "Lie on your side for 390 days. Then lie on your other side for forty days." (This is in Ezekiel 4.) Ezekiel's life for more than a year illustrated years of rebellion against God. For those who had ears to hear and eyes to see, it would have been a heart-breaking illustration. Each *day* of Ezekiel's life showed a *year* of a whole nation's rebellion. No wonder God was heart-broken.

For those who have ears to hear and eyes to see, Lent is a prophetic act, illustrated words. We give up something to have room on our agenda for God. We leave space to listen. For forty days we practice orienting our attention away from something else and toward God.

As we keep Lent, we don't have to work hard to imagine what it's like to be a prophet. We discover that we are a living metaphor, a truth-teller. We begin to feel the resistance of those unwilling to change themselves. We become the messenger that people want to shoot.

2 .The danger of the successful prophet

Elijah was a prophet.

He suddenly appears in 1 Kings 17, telling the king of Israel, Ahab, that the dew and the rain will not come again until he, Elijah, says so. And then he disappears from public for about three years. During that time out of the public eye, he first lives by a wilderness stream and then has a room in the house of a widow. In both places food is provided in miraculous ways.

Elijah's action feels abrupt, until we see that Moses predicted this very thing. In Deuteronomy, Moses's last lecture at the edge of the Promised Land, he warns:

"Be careful, or you will be enticed to turn away and worship other gods and bow down to them. Then the Lord's anger will burn against you, and He will shut the heavens so that it will not rain and the ground will yield no produce, and you will soon perish from the good land the Lord is giving you." (Deuteronomy 11:16-17).

Before Ahab, king after king allowed the people to worship other gods, to cover all their deity options. There had been prophets before Elijah, warning the kings and the people. But Ahab was the worst: *"There was never a man like Ahab, who sold himself to do evil in the eyes of the Lord, urged on by Jezebel his wife."* (1 Kings 21:25). As God's response to Ahab's behavior, Elijah appears, says that the heavens will be shut, and then disappears.

When Elijah shows up in public after three years, he meets again with King Ahab. He tells Ahab that it's time to decide which god is real: the fertility god, Baal, that Ahab's wife Jezebel has been worshipping, or the Lord, the God of Israel. Elijah invites Ahab to a showdown on Mount Carmel. Two altars. Two sacrificial bulls. Two gods. The being who sends fire and lights the altar is the winner, is *The God.*

The prophets of Baal build an altar. They spend a whole day praying for fire. Nothing happens.

As evening approaches, Elijah builds an altar with twelve stones. He digs a trench around it. He pours so much water over it that the wood is soaked and the trench is full. And then he says,

"O Lord, God of Abraham, Isaac and Israel, let it be known today that you are God in Israel and that I am your servant and have done all these things at your command. Answer me, O Lord, answer me, so these people will know that you, O Lord, are God, and that you are turning their hearts back again." (1 Kings 18:36-37)

Fire comes. The wood, the bulls, the water, the stones and the soil are burned up. The people worship God. They capture and execute the false prophets. Elijah watches for rain. When a small cloud appears, he warns King Ahab to hurry home before the storm. And Elijah runs faster than the chariot back to Jezreel, Ahab's capital.

And when Jezebel hears the news, she warns Elijah that she will kill him. And after all Elijah's experiences of God's protection and provision over the previous three years, he is afraid. He runs for his life. Ninety miles to Beersheba. Another day into the wilderness. A simple prayer: "I have had enough, Lord. Take my life." And a deep, exhausted sleep.

3. Simply being zealous doesn't impress God

When Elijah woke up, he saw an angel. Exactly what a prophet who asks to die wants to see. But he wasn't dead. So Elijah decided to go to the mountain of God. He needed to talk to God.

At the beginning of Elijah's journey, an angel fixed him breakfast. Sometimes we are just hungry, and God knows that. Sometimes we just need sleep. And God knows that.

But sometimes, even after the breakfast, we are still on a journey. For Elijah, at the end of his journey is the mountain of God. In between was forty days spent alone.

That's what the life of following Jesus feels like. A supernatural start. A future hope. And in between is wilderness. The wild places past the last homely house.

I suppose that God could have talked to Elijah along the way. But sometimes we have to travel a long way to be alone with God. Sometimes it takes forty days for our frustration to become clear.

By the end of the journey, standing on the mountain of God, Elijah's lament had clarified.

"I have been very zealous for the LORD God Almighty. The Israelites have rejected your covenant, broken down your altars, and put your prophets to death with the sword. I am the only one left, and now they are trying to kill me, too." (1 Kings 19:10)

It's possible for us to spend our entire Lenten journey working on our speech for God. We keep track of when the prayer feels mechanical. When we are hungry because of following God, and the relationships we are praying for are still messed up, and the wisdom we want for our future still isn't available. Day after day of hunger. Day after day of silence. Day after day we distill our lament until it fits on a 3x5 card, or can be recited on an elevator ride.

God says, "So why are you here?"

And we say, "I have been very zealous for you. Everyone else is rejecting you and killing your people. I'm the only one left. And now they are after me. When are you going to pay attention to me?"

4. God invites Elijah into conversation

We have pictures of God. Sometimes on our wall. Always in our minds.

So did Elijah.

I'm guessing that's why God provided a wind that shattered rocks and an earthquake that sifted the shattered rocks into a new landscape and a fire that purified that landscape of vegetation. Elijah wanted to see power, a response that would match the pain of his lonely lament.

"Make them pay. Vindicate me."

But God wasn't in the wind or the earthquake or the fire. He was behind them, causing them, but they weren't *him*.

You can lean into wind, but you can't reason with it. You can be warmed by fire, but you can't converse with it. You can recognize the power behind an earthquake, but you can't complain to it. And God is, by nature, relationship. Not just relational. A God in three persons is the essence of relationship. That's why we read that God is love. By coming to Elijah in a quiet whisper, God is inviting Elijah into that relationship.

"What are you doing here, Elijah?"

God knew the answer. He didn't need to ask. But He did anyway.

God comes to us where we are. He allows us to argue with him, to complain to him. He won't let us get away with wrong facts, and He corrects us in his presence and with compassion.

5. When you are sent, the sender is everything

I heard God talk to me once. He said, "It's okay, son. Go to bed." Elijah's message was less comforting:

"Go back. Anoint the replacement for King Ahab. Anoint

the replacement for the neighboring king. And anoint Elisha as your replacement. And there are 7,000 people just like you, people who have not rejected me." (1 Kings 19:15-18)

It's a blunt message. God says, "The end of your work is on the horizon, Elijah. You are being replaced. You can't see the facts, Elijah. Go do something that will aggravate Jezebel more than anything you could imagine, Elijah."

But Elijah's assignment is given in the context of relationship. God isn't angry with him. God isn't sending him away from his presence. In fact, God esteems Elijah. At the end of his life, Elijah's life doesn't end. A chariot of fire comes and takes him away. The Old Testament ends talking about Elijah. An angel starts the New Testament by talking to John the Baptist's dad about Elijah.

I don't know what your message is. I don't know what God wants to tell you through this Lenten journey. If I did, you wouldn't need the journey. But I am confident that whatever your speech when you get to the mountain of God, He will talk with you.

6. A habit of conversation: I asked if Jesus would like tea

I had two hours alone at home. It was quiet. I could work. Except I couldn't.

I was distracted.

I decided to stop and talk with God a bit. The thoughts kept running. I kept moving.

So I asked Jesus if He would like a cup of tea. Literally. Out loud.

I went to the stove and turned on the burner under the kettle. I went upstairs to change for my lunch appointment. I thought about inviting Jesus to tea.

I remembered a story in Revelation 3 where Jesus talks about standing outside a door knocking, willing to come in and eat a bit.

I thought about the hands that picked the tea leaves, on hillsides I've never seen, watered by rains I can't control, in countries I'll never visit.

I heard the whistle of the kettle. I poured a bit of water into the mug to warm it. It was a John Deere mug, with a family of deer on it. Andrew wanted to be a farmer. That dream is gone, but he and Allie and Hope and Dan still have dreams.

I got the tea bag out of the jar on the counter, the tea I got from Diane. I thought about her gift and her family.

I added sugar and poured the water in. I thought about my mom who has often prescribed tea for headaches.

I sat in the living room, in the rocking chair where my grandfather sat.

I thought about the tense email conversation I'd had with a friend and the meeting I was going to.

I looked at the color swatches on the sofa and thought about the tension that sometimes comes in decorating.

I tasted the hot sweet tea, and my eyes began to fill with tears.

And I knew that I was drinking tea with Jesus.

7. Reflections on Sabbath from playing the tuba

I used to play the tuba. Tuba players learn to wait. There are often long stretches of the music during which the wind ensemble plays and we don't. We spend these times counting very carefully (1-2-3-4, 2-2-3-4, 3-2-3-4 and so on). It is stressful at times. You have a loud instrument. You have to enter at the right place.

One night a friend was talking about this very experience. He plays trumpet, his son is a violinist, and both spend time resting and counting.

As Kent talked about this kind of resting, he mentioned the challenge of learning to rest in the resting, to be able to enjoy what other people are doing, to enjoy the music.

When we are resting, we give other people the opportunity to be heard. A tuba covers up a lot.

When we rest, the clarinets can be heard more clearly. And sometimes, they need to be featured that way.

When we are resting, we are reminded that we don't have to play all the time to make a meaningful contribution to the piece. The silence is part of the playing as well.

When we are resting, we can be preparing for the playing that we do.

I suppose that there may be some application of these ideas outside of music. But I'll stop playing and let you think about it.

WEEK 4: LENT AS LIVING LIKE JESUS

The most famous forty-day fast is the one Jesus had. After his baptism, before his ministry starts, Jesus spends forty days in the wilderness. This time of self-denial, culminating in the most focused temptation we can imagine, gives us a model of living like Jesus. Matthew describes it in Matthew 4.

1. Fasting is not penance, it's preparation

Jesus always went away from people to pray before big events. He went away before choosing the twelve. He went away before moving from his adopted hometown of Capernaum. It was his way of getting ready. Spending time with the Father gave him strength, kept him focused. Before He went public with his preaching, He took a longer than normal time away. This time it was forty days.

We have no idea what, exactly, He did during those forty days. Apart from not eating. What we do know is that at the end of that time He was hungry.

You may be thinking, "Of course He was hungry. Who wouldn't be hungry after a forty-day fast?" But it's less obvious than we think. The claim the Bible makes is that Jesus is God *and* human. That He is the son of God *and* the son of man. If He wasn't human, completely human, He wouldn't get hungry no matter how long He didn't eat. So the human part by definition requires that He got hungry, that He *wanted* to eat, that He *needed* to eat, that He *could* eat.

But the God part shows us the nature of fasting. The fact that Jesus fasted means that fasting doesn't make a person perfect. He already was. It doesn't make a person more acceptable to God. He already was. It doesn't make a person better. He already was.

Fasting is about preparation.

2. Preparation can take a long time.

The heavens parted.

We use that phrase jokingly when someone is about to make some dramatic pronouncement. In the situation that Matthew talks about in Matthew 3:13-4:11, there *was* a dramatic pronouncement. Though not a joke, it feels pretty friendly. The heavens part, the dove descends, and the Father says of the Son, "I'm proud of him."

While that warm feeling lingers, the scene changes. Jesus is led out into the desert. Jesus doesn't eat for forty days and nights. Satan shows up and suggests that Jesus make some bread out of the rocks.

We look at the story, and we cheer for Jesus. We talk about how well He resists the temptation to turn the well-baked stones into no-need-to-bake loaves. We cheer when He quotes Deuteronomy to the devil.

But our optimism comes from looking at the story from 40,000 feet, long after the forty days are over. We've got to look at it from ground level.

Jesus gets a divine affirmation of his identity. What He already knew to be true is stated with a voice from heaven and a descending dove. It's heard by his cousin, John, and whoever else was around. From a human perspective, a public affirmation by your dad is about as big an affirmation as you can get.

Then Jesus is directed to the desert. There is no food. And the next day, no food. And the next day, no food and the next day and the next. When He had stayed in the desert for as long as Elijah traveled through the desert, the devil showed up.

It's a story that looks just like Elijah: big emotional high, long period of dryness, big confrontation.

It sounds exactly like the lives of many people I know. Just when they think that God loves them, stuff blows up. And they wonder where the love is.

But God's love isn't measured by the length of time between spectacles.

Relationship never is.

Jesus understands the long wait. From the inside.

3. The devil says "jump" when we're hungry
Matthew says the devil told Jesus to jump from the temple

wall. That's the highest point on the spiritual center of the holy city. It's posed as a challenge: "If you are the Son of God," he said, "throw yourself down. For it is written: 'He will command his angels concerning you, and they will lift you up in their hands, so that you will not strike your foot against a stone.'" (Matthew 4:6)

You know the thing mothers used to say? When you say that *everyone* is doing something, they are supposed to say, "If everyone was jumping off a cliff, would you jump?" We know enough to not respond to that kind of peer pressure. We have brains.

But what if 'everyone' quotes the Bible? When the devil says to jump, he's quoting Psalm 91. That's pretty authoritative, right? So if the Bible says "jump", then we should jump.

But the Bible doesn't say to jump, particularly not in the passage the devil quotes. The passage is about protection in the face of adversity, not willful leaping from tall buildings for the sake of defending God.

"What?" you say. "For the sake of defending God? Where is that in the text?"

The devil quotes scripture. The implication is, if you really believe in God, you will do this. Otherwise, you prove that you don't really believe God, that you don't trust him, that you aren't really a follower. You have to jump to defend God.

It's a familiar feeling. When a person who lies about everything accuses someone of not being very Christian, what, exactly, does that mean? When a person unfamiliar with any of the Bible says, "Aren't you supposed to love everyone? So why are you not helping me?" what exactly, does that mean? When the challenge is one sentence with no context but an argument, the best approach is to do what Jesus does.

Jesus faced challenges starting with "But it's in the Bible" all his life. So do we. Look at how Jesus responds to the devil with a different passage, one used accurately: "It is also written: 'Do not put the Lord your God to the test.'" (Matthew 4:7 quoting Deuteronomy 6:16.)

In that response, Jesus gives us a principle: *read the whole book.*

4. And Jesus says, "Don't test God."

Let's go back to what Jesus said to the devil about jumping. Jesus said, "It is also written, 'Do not put the Lord your God to the test.'"

Want to go exploring for a little bit?

Jesus was quoting Deuteronomy 6:16. But He left out part of the sentence. In Deuteronomy, Moses writes, "Do not test the LORD your God **as you did at Massah**." Let's keep exploring, to find out more about Massah.

Deuteronomy 6 refers back to a story told in Exodus 17. We know the Israelites were on their way from Egypt to Mount Sinai. But they didn't know where, exactly, they were going; they just knew they were following fire and a cloud. They discovered they had come to a place where there wasn't any water. So they grumbled and quarreled with Moses.

Moses tells them to trust God. The God who brought them out of Egypt. The God who made a path through the sea. The God who had given them food, with very precise instructions that showed them He would provide for them if they trusted.

But trusting wasn't what they did. They grumbled.

And Moses said, "Why do you put God to the test?"

God was testing their faith in Him. He was giving them an opportunity to trust Him. But rather than trusting, the Israelites created a test for *him*: "Give us water or we will question whether you are really God."

The place got named "testing", *Massah*. Forty years later Moses says to the people, "Don't test God like at Massah." And several centuries later, Jesus says to the devil, we're not supposed to test God like at Massah. And two millennia later, we read it and think, "Am I setting relational traps for God to prove He loves me?"

5. Fasting means giving up nothing for everything.

There must have been binoculars on the top of the mountain where the devil took Jesus, those tourist binoculars. You put some quarters in. A shutter opens inside the huge, odd-shaped, metal blob. You look through the eyepieces and see a portion of the beauty in front of the vantage point. You may hear a soft ticking sound as a timer eats through the money. And then, suddenly, everything goes black.

You don't own what you see, you just rent a view of it. You only see what the person installing the binoculars wants you to see. You can't look behind you. You can't pick them up and follow a bird flying or those kids playing.

A limited view of infinity for a few quarters.

That was the deal the devil was trying to make with Jesus. From the mountain there was an astonishing view. "All the kingdoms of the world and their splendor," we read. All of that for a mere touching of the knee to the ground. Everything for nothing was the offer. Because worship is cheap.

The truth? The offer was *nothing* for *everything*. Stuff doesn't matter. Relationship matters completely. The devil was willing to give up all the stuff of the world to get a relationship with Jesus. As long as the devil came out on top.

Who you have a relationship with makes all the difference. The relationship that Jesus affirms is not with the devil. Jesus declares dismissively, "Away from me, Satan! For it is written: 'Worship the Lord your God, and serve him only.'"

Often, we are offered binocular views of shiny objects with a similar offer: just touch your knee to the ground. And if worship is cheap enough to us, that deal seems simple.

And wrong.

+++

"Then the devil left him, and angels came and attended him." (Matthew 4: 11)

6. Being prepared means preparing

The way to have responses to problems is to learn about them ahead of time. To quote Deuteronomy to the devil, you have to actually know Deuteronomy. And that happens through regular preparation.

Many people have memorized the Bible. Most people who watch sporting events have memorized John 3:16, for example. The reference at least.

But that doesn't mean they know what it means.

Some people have memorized parts of the Bible. From phrases to sentences to paragraphs to pages to whole books, people have memorized the Bible.

But that doesn't mean they know what it means.

Some people teach other people about the Bible. They can talk about how many books there are, how many versions have been written. They can talk about how many authors may have written which books of the Bible. They can speak with great confidence.

But that doesn't mean they know what it means.

Some people can study in several languages. They have learned Greek and Hebrew and Aramaic and Latin. They can explain how the tenses of a particular verb were translated incorrectly by that group. As a result, they tell us, we have all been wrong for the last 1900 years about what Jesus really meant.

But that doesn't mean they know what it means.

Jesus was forty days into a fast. He was hungry. He needed

food. Not wanted, needed. And forty days into this fast, the devil shows up to test him, to show him what it feels like to be human.

The devil reminds Jesus that Jesus has the power to turn stones into bread. (As will be seen later, Jesus could take five dinner rolls and feed 15,000 people.)

And Jesus says, "It is written: 'Man does not live on bread alone, but on every word that comes from the mouth of God.'" (Matthew 4:4)

In the face of adversity, remembering and saying and living even one sentence God told us counts as knowing what it means.

Jesus knew.

7. Our Sabbath group

Most Saturday nights, a dozen of us get together in the church basement. Two or three people bring the meal. Mostly comfort food. Someone from the family that brings the meal thanks God for the food and the time together. And then we eat, gathered around a long table. We take an hour or so, conversations merging into one and then splitting apart again.

We laugh. We go back for seconds. We share life.

We move our circle slowly to a cluster of sofas. We talk about how we can help a couple people who need help with a porch, with getting to college. And then we dig into the implications of the sermon we heard the week before. We wrestle with how to make something a habit, with what Jesus really meant when He said that, with why we feel so trapped by perfectionism when God talks about grace.

It takes about ninety minutes to exhaust the handful of questions in front of us, ninety minutes to let others see our struggles, our souls, our dilemmas, our faith. And then we take another twenty minutes, after we are officially done, to finally say goodbye. And we go home.

The next morning, most of us are in the same building. We see each other with a smile, aware that Sunday actually started Saturday night, that church isn't just what looks like a concert and lecture, it's the life we shared on Saturday night. And the projects we've done for other people.

We started years ago "just for six weeks." Now we can't stop.

It's not complicated, by the way. It starts with "Are you hungry? For supper and God?"

And goes from there.

WEEK 5: LENT AS FINDING LIVING FOOD

The stories of Jesus can be summarized simply. For example, in a story from John 4, Jesus wants to talk with a thirsty woman without questions from the loyal, but annoying, disciples. The woman's life is transformed. The disciples are confused. And a whole town is changed. Read on.

1. Jesus wants to talk

Jesus was heading to Galilee—to home.

He was heading away from Jerusalem, away from controversy with religious people. In the process, He walks right into the middle of religious controversy.

He had to go through Samaria.

Samaritans were regarded by Jews as half-breeds, as spiritual wanna-bes. Jews were regarded by Samaritans as uppity, as arrogant, as holier-than-thou.

I tried to think of a way to imagine that trip. Here's as close as I can get. It would be like a Catholic priest walking into Protestant bar in Northern Ireland during the Troubles and asking for a drink. Religion, politics, prejudice.

Jesus, of course, knew exactly what He was doing. He wasn't looking for trouble. He didn't want to start a fight. He wanted to start a conversation. He went to Samaria and stopped by a well and sent his disciples into town for food *because* He knew a woman was coming to get water, and He wanted to talk with her.

Ah, but that's a problem, too. A Jewish man talking with a Samaritan woman. And a rabbi at that.

What would people think? What would people say? What would it do to his reputation if anyone found out?

Jesus didn't care much about what people thought. He cared about people. He cared about this particular woman that no one else cared much about. He made the conversation simple by sitting at a well that would provide a common point of conversation.

And the topic? Genealogy and water.

This was Jacob's well. The same Jacob that was renamed Israel. The same Jacob who was ancestor to the Samaritans and Jews.

Jesus met her exactly where she was living. He didn't make her come to where He was living. And He asked her for help.

I'm pretty sure He still works that way. Starting conversations with us on our way through life.

2. With a thirsty woman

And Jesus said, "Can I have a drink of water?"

The woman can't believe He's asking.

Jesus says, "If you knew more about me, you'd be asking me for a drink. Of living water."

Jesus makes an unusual claim, and she attempts to figure out what it means. She responds, in order: 1) You have nothing to draw water with. 2) The well is deep. 3) Where is living water? 4) Are you better than Jacob, our ancestor, who actually watered generations of sheep from this well? Her responses to Jesus were practical, historical, and appropriate.

Jesus differentiates between regular water and living water. With living water you won't get thirsty. In fact, you will end up with a spring inside that will make you live forever.

That's as peculiar as it sounds. Unless, of course, you are Jesus. And you are sitting next to a well in the middle of the morning talking to someone who is coming to the well at a time different than everyone else, perhaps because she is looking for something that will satisfy a deeper thirst.

This unnamed woman, after all, remains involved in the conversation with Jesus. How can we tell? Because she wants some of that water, that soul-satisfying, thirst-quenching, free-flowing water. She asks for it.

It's easy to forget, steeped in millennia of church as we are, lost in structures and steeples and sanctuaries and ceremonies, that Jesus wasn't selling or recruiting or promoting. He wasn't convincing or conniving or cajoling.

He was offering what people wanted, deep down, but never hoped that they would actually find.

And He did it without scolding.

How do we know? Because of where the woman's part of this story goes next.

But, while we wait for that turn, just a thought:

What are you thirsty for?

3. Without annoying disciples

It's time to step back and look at the disciples.

"Rabbi, you look tired. You need something to eat. Here, sit by this well. We'll go into that little town. It looks safe enough, for a Samaritan city. Maybe just some of us should go, and some of us should stay. No? Okay, I don't know about this, but you're the rabbi. Just don't pray the whole time. Judas, you got the money?"

I think Jesus was as glad to have them gone as to have food coming.

"Guys, you go on into town. No, all of you. I'll be fine here by myself. I've got some thinking to do. No, it's okay. Just go. If you don't leave you won't get back."

Jesus wanted to talk about living water with the woman who came to the well.

Then the disciples get back.

"Wait, how'd she get here?"

"Shhh."

"But why is He talking with..."

"Shhh!"

"But what will everyone ..."

"SHHH!"

"Jesus, now that we're *alone*, how about some lunch? It wasn't much of a town, but we did some great bargaining and wouldn't let them get the better of us. We've got some dried fish, and some rolls, just out of the oven. In fact, we could have been back here sooner so you wouldn't have to be *alone* if we hadn't had to wait. But now we're here, and we'll take care of you, so here. Eat."

Jesus says He's eaten.

"How did you eat? Why didn't you wait for us? Did you do the bread and fish thing again? Here we are trying to help you, and we discover you are sending us of on a wild goose chase."

Sometimes the reason God sends us on trips is not to get food. It's to get us out of the way. Our presence can prevent his conversations.

4. The woman's life was transformed

The woman runs into town.

"Come and see! Come and see!"

No one looks up. She's fallen in and out of love so many times that no one much cares what she says. Her judgment about what is worth looking at is, shall we say, questionable.

"I think I might have found the Christ."

You can imagine what is running through minds along the street. "That's what you are calling him now?" "Isn't that a stretch, even for you?"

"He's told me everything I ever did."

The people stopped.

This is a woman married five times. This is a woman keeping house again. This is a woman with a denial addiction. This is a woman who goes to get water when no one else will be at the well, no one to ask questions, to point. This is a woman with a gaping hole in her self. This is a woman who says, "This time it will be different. This time I've changed. Forget all the rest of those times. This time, it will work."

This is the woman who comes running into town demanding attention, finally admitting to everyone that there really has been trouble in her life. Her invitation is to come and meet the man who saw her heart and still conversed with her.

Her work as an evangelist was powerful. The people from the village stopped what they were doing and followed her to Jesus. Not because she was perfect and polished and newly successful but because, for the first time they could remember, she told the truth about herself.

Makes you wonder, doesn't it, about why many of us who call ourselves Christians think we need to be perfect before talking to Jesus, before talking about Jesus? And why that doesn't seem to work so well?

Maybe we just need to be honest about ourselves.

5. The disciples are confused

Jesus is sitting on the edge of a well. His disciples are standing around him. They are holding sandwiches. He is holding forth.

"Do you know," He says, "what fills my belly more than

those sandwiches you are holding? Do you know what makes me get up in the morning, what so captivates me that I don't even notice when I'm hungry? Do you know why I am so focused when I'm in a conversation that matters? *My food is to do the will of him who sent me and to finish his work.*

"You know how you say, 'We've got plenty of time. No need to hurry. The harvest isn't coming for four months.' You, dear friends, are fooling yourselves. Look at the fields. They are ripe."

At which point, the disciples would have begun to nudge each other. Jesus may have been a great rabbi, but He was a lousy farmer. The fields around the disciples couldn't have been ripe.

If they *had* been ripe, the disciples each could have grabbed a handful of grain. By law, if they were hungry, they could have snacked as they walked. And Jesus, knowing their thoughts, may well have laughed out loud at that point.

"Open your eyes! Look! The fields are white with harvest."

As they grudgingly turned around, they would have seen what Jesus saw. Bobbing along the path from the village, looking for all the world like waves of wheat, were the white robes and tanned faces and curly hair of the people coming to find out what the woman had been talking about.

"Sometimes," Jesus says, "all you have to do is show up. Stop trying to do everything. Be glad that you are part of a team. The conversation may come to you. The questions may come to you. And I'm here, too."

6. A whole town is changed

No one in Israel would have said that the person to point people to a rabbi would be a Samaritan adulteress.

The only people she would have been able to lead anywhere were people who knew her and saw what that rabbi had done for her.

People in and out of church know all about evangelism. People inside know the gut-wrenching fear of having to walk up to some random house, knock on the door, and say, "God loves you and has a wonderful plan for your life," or "Do you know where you would spend eternity if you died tonight?" or "What kind of church would you be interested in if you could design it?" or some other script taught by well-meaning evangelism instructors. People outside know the sheer confusion of having someone knock on their door and say, "Goddowhatlovesyoukindyouknowofandwherechurchhell?"

You can fill in your own stories of pain and fear and confusion and annoyance, of "bait and switch" and direct marketing and being a notch in someone's belt. And even the terms "inside" and "outside" hurt.

In the ending to the story about the Samaritan adulteress, the people from her village talk about why they decided to follow Jesus.

"At first we came to see him because we couldn't believe how He had made you an honest woman. Then we couldn't believe that He actually was willing to stay with us for two whole days (a Jew in our ceremonially unclean village). And then we listened to what He said, about us, about God, about himself."

They said to the woman, "We no longer believe just because of what you said; now we have heard for ourselves, and we know that this man really is the Savior of the world" (John 4:42).

Relationships. First with her, then with him. That's what living water and God's-will bread can restore.

7. A Sabbath reflection: Jesus working on the Sabbath

Jesus told a man to pick up his mat and walk. The man did. He picked up the mat and walked, right into the attention of the religious leaders.

Jesus disappeared into the crowd. When asked, the man didn't even know the name of the man who had told him to do the unimaginable.

A few pages later, we find Jesus putting mud on a man's eyes and sending him to wash it off. The man, who couldn't see, knew it was Jesus but didn't have any idea what He looked like.

In both cases, the men are subjected to Pharisaical interrogation. The authorities are worried, by the way, with technical obedience of the law. The healings happen on the Sabbath, the day of rest, the day laden with behavior rules.

"The man who healed me told me to carry this mat," the man said.

What right did the healer have to tell him to carry his mat, to disobey the law on the Sabbath? He was the healer, the one who brought freedom after 38 years. To the now-walking man it was self-evident.

The men can't explain the spiritual how of the healing. They know they are well, and they say as much; but then they cannot give a satisfactory account of the healing to the authorities, to the skeptics.

Why does Jesus heal these men and then leave them dangling without details?

Faith wasn't necessary for the healing, not much anyway. They didn't do anything to earn it, to deserve it, to make it happen.

But now that they are healed, will they be willing to tell what little they know about what happened? Or will they look for other explanations, for other reasons, for other understanding?

These men told what they knew. And for that, they were given more. They saw Jesus.

(The story of the man and the mat is in John 5. The story of the blind man is in John 9.)

WEEK 6: LENT AS PREPARATION FOR THE FEAST

Jesus brought Lazarus back from the dead. That's the action part of the story. But the conversation part of the story teaches us about how to talk with Jesus, how to live our personalities, how to face death and life. It helps if we remember that conversations with Jesus count as prayer, if we remember that prayer is talking to Jesus. This story unfolds a few days before Jesus was captured. It's told in John 11. Look carefully at the faces around the table at this feast. You may see one familiar from the mirror.

1. Not permanently dead

When Jesus heard that his friend Lazarus was sick, He said 'This sickness will not end in death." (John 11:4) It's an odd statement, given that the only thing that He had been told was, "Lord, the one you love is sick." There is no word in the story about how sick Lazarus was. There is no sense, for sure, that he was on his way to death.

Jesus waited for a couple days and then headed toward

Bethany, where Lazarus was. It was also toward Jerusalem, a city with leaders wanting to have Jesus dead. By the time Jesus showed up, traveling a couple days' distance, Lazarus had been entombed for four days.

There are many stories in this story. We see that Martha (of Mary and Martha fame) isn't nearly as unspiritual as many people try to make her. We hear Thomas (of doubting Thomas fame) being willing to walk into death. We see Jesus weeping. We hear Jesus calling Lazarus out of the grave.

This story is a crossroads of characters. I've known this story as far back as I can remember. But I don't remember ever seeing that Jesus said, *"This sickness will not end in death."*

Why would Jesus say that? I mean, a couple days later, still not on the road, Jesus says, "Lazarus is dead." Why can't He get his story straight?

It's possible, of course, that his story was straight, that the sickness didn't **end** in death; the sickness just had to make a stop at death on the way to healing.

This can be a scary story for people who ask Jesus for help. Who could ever trust someone who would let good friends watch a brother die, only to have him brought back to life? To our eyes, that looks like random infliction of pain.

On the other hand, Jesus knew that death wasn't fatal. At least not for Lazarus. Not the first time he died.

2. A simple conversation with Jesus

Sermons are long, unbroken stretches of words. Conversations are short, choppy exchanges of words. Sometimes Jesus offers sermons. Often, He uses conversations.

In John 11, we read a conversation between Jesus and Martha. Her brother has just died. When she meets Jesus at the edge of town, she is pretty direct: "If you had been here," she said, "my brother would not have died."

It wasn't like Jesus didn't know her brother was sick. She had sent Him a message days before. There had been time.

We know (though she didn't) that Jesus had deliberately waited until her brother had died. Martha knew that if Jesus arrived while Lazarus was on his deathbed, there was time to heal his body. There was time to take his hand and lift him to health, to touch his forehead, to speak a word of health. Martha even knew that Jesus had raised little girls and only sons from the dead. But in each of those cases death had visited only hours before. And Jesus stayed away until it was too late, until Lazarus started to decay in the heat.

Martha calmly confronts Jesus with the truth. "If you had been here," she said, "my brother would not have died."

"Your brother will rise again," Jesus said.

She took it as a familiar theological affirmation: "I know he will rise again in the resurrection at the last day."

But Jesus wasn't going to let her be that vague. Jesus said to her, "I am the resurrection and the life. He who believes in me will live, even though he dies; and whoever lives and believes in me will never die. Do you believe this?"

It is a clear, simple statement of what Jesus does, who Jesus is. To a grieving, yet hopeful, sister, it was the message that she wanted to hear. Shorter than a sermon, and more comforting.

Her answer was, in paraphrase, "I believe you are the Christ, the Messiah."

Then Jesus called a dead Lazarus out of a grave.

This is a message perfectly suited to this audience, stated with startling simplicity and confidence, backed by incredible customer service.

In the centuries since, Jesus's followers have often taken Martha's position: "Of course there will be life after everything." Then, we've complicated the message with caveats and cautions and defenses.

Maybe Jesus is still simply right. Even though we die, we will live.

3. Sometimes Jesus prayed as performance

Nancy and I talk often. After more than thirty years together, we have developed the patterns of interaction that work for us. We walk and talk. We text. We chat on Facebook. We email.

Sometimes, when we are out for supper, we look like the couples who never talk. We eat. We listen. We look sideways at the people who are talking loudly at adjacent tables. We feel no need to perform.

Sometimes we talk in front of other people so that they *can* hear us talk, so they know how we interact. When we've been with our kids, we have made sure that we have talked and laughed and even kissed. It hasn't been made up, it's not pretend. It's the public version of a deep private relationship. We know there is an audience. We know that the audience shapes the conversation. More importantly, we know the audience is influenced by the conversation.

Jesus stood outside the tomb containing the body of Lazarus. He looked up and said,

"Father, I thank you that you have heard me. I knew that you always hear me, but I said this for the benefit of the people standing here, that they may believe that you sent me."(John 11:40-41)

With a crowd of people listening, Jesus demonstrated and described His relationship with God. He acknowledges that they talk all the time. He wants everyone to be sure that what is going to follow, Lazarus walking out of a tomb, is clearly rooted in the conversational relationship Jesus has with His father. The power to heal is not His own power. It's not a coincidence. It needs to be that Jesus made a seemingly heretical claim, and instead of being struck by lightening, Lazarus is struck by life.

Maybe like Jesus, just as I "public talk" with Nancy, I need to "public talk" with God.

4. Different sisters, different prayer

Martha calmly conversed. Mary dissolved in tears.

Two sisters, same dead brother. They both talked with Jesus, each with a different style.

After Lazarus died and Martha heard that Jesus was in town, she went and talked with him.

"Lord, if you had been here, my brother would not have died."

They had a conversation, Jesus and Martha taking turns. There is challenge and explanation. It is logical, as much as talking about resurrection can be logical. Martha asserts *what* she believes and *that* she believes.

It is, in short, a very *Martha* conversation.

Martha heads back home and tells Mary that Jesus wants to talk with her. Mary goes to him, leading a crowd of friends and mourners.

"Lord, if you had been here, my brother would not have died."

Mary starts her conversation with Jesus, her prayer, exactly the same way Martha did. Then Mary dissolves into a weeping bundle at Jesus's feet.

Jesus, the text says, "was deeply moved and troubled in spirit."

Jesus and Mary go to the grave.

"Jesus wept."

We can suggest that Jesus was weeping the loss of Lazarus, that He was grieving his own death just days away. But I wonder.

These two interactions with these two women are perfectly suited to what we know of the women. The sense of perfectly appropriate response is genius, pure emotionally intelligent genius.

What if Jesus had switched his response, weeping with Martha, teaching Mary? It would feel wrong, rude, somehow. It would lack any sense that He really knew these women, knew their hearts, their personalities. Instead, He interacts with Martha and weeps with Mary and each has a sense that Jesus really knows them.

I wonder how often we miss the conversation and comfort Jesus offers. We look for some formal religiosity. We seek someone else's formula for spiritual success. Meanwhile, He's waiting to converse. Or cry.

5. The dinner party

There was a dinner party in Bethany.

It was like the meal after any funeral, I suppose, full of stories about the person who had died. The family was around, friends of the family were there. Unlike every funeral meal I've been part of, the person who had died was listening to the stories. And the guest of honor wasn't the formerly dead person.

I'm guessing people asked Lazarus what it had been like to be dead. I'm guessing they looked at Jesus out of the corner of their eyes as Lazarus talked. No one exactly wanted to ask Jesus how the healing happened. I mean, you don't come out and say, "Whoa, how'd you do *that?*" If He *was* the son of God, you'd be kind of scared. If He *wasn't* the son of God, you'd be kind of scared, too. (Think first century zombies.)

So everyone at the party would have been excited and curious and awestruck and nervous. People wouldn't quite know what to do.

Except for three people.

Lazarus was at the table, sitting with Jesus. Martha was serving. And Mary was by Jesus's feet.

That sounds like another story, told over in Luke 10. These same three people were doing similar things. Lazarus was at the table, Martha was getting food ready, Mary was by Jesus's feet. And Martha was ticked.

"Lord, tell Mary to help!" she said.

"Martha, relax. Mary has chosen the better thing."

Too often, people have taught that we are all supposed to stop rushing around and sit at Jesus's feet, just like Mary. And we feel guilty because we are not being devoted to Jesus the same way really spiritual people are, like Mary. But the dinner party story says we got the lesson wrong. Cooking isn't unspiritual. As long as Jesus is the guest of honor.

6. Silent Lazarus

I just realized something. Lazarus never *says* anything.

I mean, Martha and Mary both have speaking roles in more than one story. They both talk with Jesus, Martha several times. But Lazarus? Never a word.

The more I think about it, he never *does* much of anything, either. First he dies. Then, when Jesus tells him to come out of the tomb, he walks out. With his legs wrapped and face covered, that probably wasn't too smooth. Then, at the banquet for Jesus celebrating Lazarus's resurrection, he's just sitting there (or, as they say, "reclining at the table.")

For all his trouble, Lazarus gets included as a target in the plot to kill Jesus. Many people were trying to see him ("See the man, once dead, now walking") and were realizing that Jesus had done something amazing ("I want to know that Guy"). The leaders decided that he had to die, too ("Maybe he'll *stay* dead this time.")

We're laughing a bit at his utter passivity, but I'm realizing that there is nothing that Lazarus could say that would be nearly as compelling as his sheer presence. Apart from some interesting insights into what it would be like to be dead ("I saw a bright light. I started walking toward it." "Wow! Did you see God?" "Absolutely. As soon as they took the cloth off my face, I looked right at him."), what of significance could he say other than, "I was dead. Jesus spoke. I was alive."?

I'm thinking that dead people walking would still be compelling. Dead marriages growing, dead dreams waking, dead relationships forgiving, dead churches breathing.

I have a feeling that there is still a voice saying, "Lazarus (and you and you) come out."

I'm curious, though. Could he have said, "I'm comfortable dead, I don't want the Pharisees to kill me"?

7. And then the last week came

Apparently, we don't need to know what Jesus did on His last Sabbath before His death and resurrection. Because we aren't told. We know what happens the next day. The next day is Palm Sunday. The next day is the beginning of intense preaching, massive arguments, political intrigue. Before the next Saturday, Jesus will be dead.

In this moment before the final week, pray a simple prayer: "Jesus, help me get ready for the feast."

WEEK 7: LENT AS REMEMBERING

During His last week before being crucified, Jesus leaves the disciples in the audience. He needs to teach them how to stand up to authority, even to the death, how to serve each other, how to remember His sacrifice, how to forgive the unforgivable. But those are lessons taught by showing more than explaining. The stories this week put Jesus in the spotlight. But we can learn to remember Jesus's sacrifice by watching the disciples watch.

1. A God who pursues.

"That's not how we do things." That's the message of status quo. Whoever *we* is, decides. And whoever *we* is, defends.

We build rules. We build penalties. We welcome. We shun. We shape whatever we can shape to keep whatever authority we can keep.

When the outsiders, the newcomers, the challengers begin to threaten our status, we will do almost anything to stop them. If the threat is great enough, and our livelihoods and lives are at risk, we may even kill the challengers.

It happens on TV shows all the time. It happens in history.

And it happened once in Jerusalem.

"If we let him go on like this, everyone will believe in him, and then the Romans will come and take away both our place and our nation."

The high council in Jerusalem had a deal with the Roman authorities: As long as the council kept the Jewish people behaving nicely, the council could keep their religious structure intact. But Jesus was threatening the structure. He was suggesting that people might not have to follow the rules the way the Pharisees taught. He was suggesting that you didn't have to be perfect to be around God. He was suggesting that God didn't sit passively waiting for people to come to him, or to the people who were his deputies.

Jesus was announcing that God was pursuing aching hearts who were clueless about how to proceed and offering them hope, comfort, healing, reconciliation, resurrection.

A God who pursues, who moves outside the building built to house Him, is a threat to the ones whose lives depended on the building. A God who moves, who treats broken people as people, not debris, will challenge empires built on debris.

No wonder the high council was ticked. Sometimes, they still are.

(This story is in John 11:47-57.)

2. "I just don't understand God"

That's what lots of people think when it comes to Jesus stuff. "I will never understand the Bible. I will never

LENT FOR NON-LENT PEOPLE

understand these stories. I will never understand God and theology."

The disciples didn't understand God and theology either. Not while they were still in the middle of the story.

How do we know? Because John tells us so. In his Gospel, John shifts between describing what Jesus did, to describing the thinking of the disciples at those moments, to describing how they ultimately understood what was happening. Sometimes the shifts feel awkward, like a person in a documentary who suddenly looks at the audience. It's like a Bible commentary that's inside the story rather than sitting on a shelf.

There is a perfect example of this perspective-shifting in John's description of Palm Sunday. In John 12, Jesus approaches Jerusalem and people formed a parade. The other writers fill in details about donkey, colt, palm branches, cloaks on the ground, people singing "Hosanna." We've heard it so often in the context of Holy Week. We think, "Wow! All this celebration and five days later they call for his death."

In John's account, he mentions Zechariah 3, the latter prefaced with "as it is written." The words didn't just *happen* to fit. They had been written about this particular parade. They weren't appropriate, they were prophetic. We could conclude that the disciples were great Bible scholars, walking through life with Jesus, understanding everything.

But they didn't. John says, "At first his disciples did not understand all this. Only after Jesus was glorified did they realize that these things had been written about him and that they had done these things to him." The disciples had no idea. They just stayed in the parade, following Jesus, hoping it would take them somewhere, wanting to understand.

Funny. Still works.

3. The disciples are not in the story

On Palm Sunday, following Jesus was pretty easy. Suddenly, Jesus was the popular one, Jesus was the celebrated one, Jesus was the one for whom everyone was cheering. After all those months of being misunderstood, of having regular attacks from all the religious leaders, now there is recognition.

It had to be interesting for the disciples. Was Jesus going to remember them now that He was a big star? Were they going to be recognized, too? Was this a big deal that Jesus set up? (After all, He had arranged for the donkey to be ready, somehow).

Wonderfully, we have no idea what they were thinking. After doing what Jesus told them to do and bringing a donkey and a colt, and after they put their coats on the colt as makeshift saddles or trappings or something, the disciples disappear into the crowd.

They aren't in the story. They aren't mentioned in the rest of Matthew 21.

I hope it was okay with them. I'm not sure it would be okay with me.

I think I want to be recognized by Jesus for my fine obedience. I think I want to be recognized for my fine colt-draping skills, for my fine coordination of the palm spectacle, for my great work handing out lyric sheets to the whole crowd so they remember their lines: "Hosanna". I think I want to be identified as one of the people who knew him as the king from way back. I think I want to be honored as part of the marching contingent, on my own float following the grand marshal.

Forgetting, of course, that I'm just called to follow.

4. Too busy for Easter

We work hard for Easter, those of us who work for churches. We plan extra services. We make services extra special. We worry about signage and supplies. We get all consumed.

We schedule Good Friday as a day off. And then many of us work. On the day that even public schools cancel classes as a religious holiday, those who are on church staff work.

I understand the pressure. I have spent years being very active for Easter services, long before I was on church staff. And I understand the anxiety of not getting it right, the fear that it (whatever it is) won't be perfect enough for all the people who are coming to church expecting to be amazed. The fear that, if we don't get it right, all those people who come to church just on Christmas and Easter will be offended or won't be impressed. And then God will be disappointed.

I was thinking through this anxiety when driving home on the Thursday of Easter week. We've worked hard. Things are ready. And I was feeling a little hollow, a little empty.

Then I started to think about Easter. The point of Easter,

the reason for Jesus dying and rising again, is that we can't get good enough. We just can't quite measure up. We always fall short when left to ourselves.

Jesus says, "Come on little weak one, and I will give you rest." It's not going to be through hard work that God is pleased, but through relationship.

Jesus says, "You can't get to the Father except through me." It's not going to be how perfectly we fit the service together, but whether we make the introductions, "Jesus, I'd like you to meet my good friend Dave. Dave, this is Jesus."

Nothing wrong with hard work. Unless we're addicted.

5. 7 lessons to learn from sleepy disciples

Some Maundy Thursday notes from Matthew 26:36-46

1. The leader keeps the vision clear, because the disciples don't. Disciples are learners. Though they know increasingly much, they still don't know everything. Jesus knew what the evening was about. The disciples didn't. It's what leaders learn to do.

2. Even earnest followers fall asleep when their stomachs are full. If you want to stay awake, you have to plan.

3. Even people close to Jesus don't always see his heart. Peter, James, and John were the disciples closest to Jesus. If anyone should have been able to read him, they should have. Matthew makes it clear that even before He left them behind to go and pray, Jesus was showing signs of anguish. But there isn't any evidence that they noticed.

4. Jesus stays in relationship with people who fall asleep when they should be praying. The first time Jesus found them sleeping, He awakened them. The second time, He let them sleep. The third time, He awakened them again because it was time to go. He wasn't angry, however. He seems to have understood. Which is important to people who fall asleep while reading the Bible. Or praying. Or writing blog posts.

5. Sometimes you don't know how close the end is going to be. The disciples fell asleep, not realizing that this was the night before Jesus was going to die. They may have assumed they would have plenty of time.

6. Jesus invited the disciples to follow His example in praying. He had gone away to pray lots of times. This time, He only goes a short way. And He encourages the disciples to pray while He is praying.

7. Jesus loved losers. Even in the hour before He's betrayed, Jesus cares for and about the disciples. Most people would despair or get angry. He doesn't.

6. Friday. Good.

There is a luxury in historical hindsight, an ability to see the lessons without going through the event. And it is that hindsight that named this morning Good. In real time, on the ground in Jerusalem, there was nothing good about spittle mixed with blood. There was nothing good about a suicidal man, remorse-ridden. There was nothing good about a group of people accepting guilt–and that momentary statement being used as the justification for generations of atrocities.

In the moment, the pain was excruciating. Had to be. Abandonment. Rejection. Nails. In the moment, there was little energy for discerning the lessons. Jesus was not working on a three point sermon, 10 lessons for a happy Good Friday, quick fashion lessons from the suffering savior ("a seamless tunic should be in everyone's closet.") No trite summaries. No cute sayings for surviving in the middle of trials ("It's Friday, but Sunday's coming.") Not even a neatly tied up blog post with some nice moral.

Just raw pain. And in the middle of it, forgiveness.

"God. How awful."

Exactly.

7. Waiting on Saturday

We know how the story turned out. We know that there was a resurrection. We know that hope was realized, that everything turned out great. We know that Sunday made up for Friday.

But on the Saturday between Good Friday and Easter Sunday, on the first of those Saturdays, on the one that happened before there was an Easter Sunday, no one on earth knew for sure what was going to happen. There had been promises, yes. There had been assurances. There had been prophecies and predictions. There was faith.

But Jesus was dead. Jesus was in the tomb. Jesus was gone.

We don't know anything about that day, about the feelings

or actions of the disciples. We know that on Sunday they were hiding. But we don't know if they went to the temple on the Sabbath.

Think about it. For the previous three years, they had spent Sabbath with Jesus. They had gone to the temple or to the synagogue. They had heard Him read, they had watched Him heal, they had listened to Him debate. The Sabbath had been a big time of activity for Jesus.

And now He's gone.

The ones in charge of the meeting places killed Him. The one who was transforming their lives had gotten Himself killed.

The disciples had to be feeling pretty uncertain about religion on that day.

We end up in that same place. We have many days in between, between our affirmations of faith and the evidences of God's action. We pray and there isn't healing yet. We hope and the job is still missing. We ache and the child is still somewhere else.

Easter Sunday tells us that God does the impossible. Easter Saturday reminds us that we are invited to live with faith.

EASTER

On the first day of the week, very early in the morning, the women took the spices they had prepared and went to the tomb. They found the stone rolled away from the tomb, but when they entered, they did not find the body of the Lord Jesus. While they were wondering about this, suddenly two men in clothes that gleamed like lightning stood beside them. In their fright the women bowed down with their faces to the ground, but the men said to them, "Why do you look for the living among the dead? He is not here; He has risen! Remember how He told you, while He was still with you in Galilee: 'The Son of Man must be delivered over to the hands of sinners, be crucified and on the third day be raised again.'" Then they remembered his words.

When they came back from the tomb, they told all these things to the Eleven and to all the others. It was Mary Magdalene, Joanna, Mary the mother of James, and the others with them who told this to the apostles. But they did not believe the women, because their words seemed to them like nonsense. Peter, however, got up and ran to the tomb. Bending over, he saw the strips of linen lying by themselves, and he went away, wondering to himself what had happened.

Luke 24: 1-12

WEEK 8: NEXT STEPS

On Easter Monday it's easy to get lost.

We have a season of fasting and focus. We end it with a huge celebration. And then we try to figure out what to do with our freedom. It's a long time until Christmas, the next big religious celebration.

In this chapter, I want to give you some next steps, some ways to carry what we've learned during Lent into the rest of the year. As our first step, let's think back about Easter.

Step one: Reflect on Easter

There's no reason to be surprised by our confusion about living after Lent, living beyond Easter. Consider the responses of people during the days following the first Resurrection day.

There are moments of sheer delight.

Mary Magdalene went to the tomb. It was empty. She went to find the disciples. She ran into Jesus on the way, first mistaking him for a gardener, then knowing the voice. She was ecstatic. Like the people who celebrate Easter with big events and great smiles. Like the people who are bubbling from the freedom. The people who thought they were dead, thought their lives were over. The people like the woman from chapter four. Easter is a reminder of everything wrong gone right.

There are moments of disbelief.

The disciples didn't think they could trust what the women said. The disciples didn't think they could believe the people from the walk to Emmaus. Thomas couldn't believe the other disciples. The people like Elijah (chapter three) who have had an amazing experience but get up the next morning and everything is normal, everything is worse than normal. The people who worked hard getting everything ready for the Easter celebration at church, hours and days and weeks. And they walk out after the Sunday services and the right rear tire is flat.

There are moments of explanation.

Two of the disciples headed out from Jerusalem on that first Sunday, full of confusion about what had happened to Jesus. They were so wrapped up with the introspection that when Jesus started walking with them, they didn't recognize him. As they walked toward Emmaus, Jesus walked through the whole Old Testament, from Moses through Jeremiah, Isaiah, Micah, and the rest. He traced the threads that pointed to him. That kind of teaching likely happened often after his resurrection.

What's so clear in the responses of the people who knew Jesus first is that they responded in different ways at different speeds. And so do we.

Step two: 33 questions to review Lent

If you want your Lenten journey to make a difference, you need to think about the journey. Set aside an hour. Turn off the connections to other people. Ask God to help you think and remember. Then, read through these questions which review the journey we've taken.

1. Why did you decide to walk though Lent this time?

2. What did you give up?

3. What did you start instead?

4. How long were you able to keep each commitment?

5. How many times did you renew those commitments?

6. After seven weeks, what habits did you find you had changed?

7. How has the routine of your life changed? Even little behaviors, thoughts.

8. What have you learned about Sabbath?

9. When you thought about Elijah walking across the wilderness for 40 days, how did that feel familiar?

10. Did you recognize the quiet voice that Elijah heard?

11. How have you understood God's ways more clearly?

12. How has God spoken to you?

13. How did you find the words of the Bible helping you change habits?

14. How did the Bible become part of your routine?

15. How did you find conversations with God becoming part of your routine?

16. How did you find food in relationship with God?

17. Who did you talk with about the gradual changes in your life?

18. Who did you talk with about God?

19. What parts of your conversations with God found their way into your conversations with other people?

20. How have you been more comfortable with silence?

21. During this season, what happened that was painful?

22. What kind of pain was it? The pain of sin? The pain of death? The pain of change? The pain of relationship change? The pain of muscles not used before? The pain of guilt? The pain of separation? The pain of restoration? The pain of being reminded of disobedience?

23. What did you say to God about that pain?

24. What kind of healing did you find? (mind? heart? body? soul?)

25. What relationships have changed because of this experience?

26. What did you learn from the story of Jesus's last days as you read the story this year?

27. What was new to you?

28. What was more raw and real to you?

29. What was more clear?

30. What do you understand even less?

31. What three things do you want to remember for the next month?

32. What changes in your life do you want to celebrate?

33. What will never change?

Step three: Relax into the new routines.

If we want our Lenten journey to make a difference, we need to relax into the routines. We need to learn to take our actions from "days in a row" to "weeks in a row" to "months in a row" to "seasons in a row."

Here's what I mean:

If you have talked with God for one day in a row, then talking with him on the next day makes it two days in a row. That is a wonderful thing. Go for three days in a row. And then seven.

If you took a Sabbath one week, taking a Sabbath day the next week makes it two weeks in a row. That is a great thing. Now go for three weeks. And then seven.

If you exercised each day for a month, then exercising on the first day of the next month means you are on your way to two months in a row. Amazing. Now go for three months. And then six.

If you spent Advent anticipating Christmas, and you spent Lent anticipating Easter, then you have been working on anticipation for two seasons in a row. Go for three by doing this exercise. And then think about Pentecost.

If you had the best Advent ever, the best Christmas ever, the best Lent ever, the best Easter ever, then you are on your way to years in a row. Look ahead to celebrating next year.

Each "in a row" helps us move toward character, toward

having a life of obedience, toward having a reputation, toward having a new routine.

We already talked about ritual and routine back in chapter two. Don't confuse the creation of new patterns in your life with making God happier with you. But notice that being known to yourself as a person who can keep commitments makes you happier with you.

Step four: 33 ways to commit to changing our faith

If we want our Lenten journey to make a difference, we need to make specific commitments.

We often think, "That's done. Back to normal." But your review of Lent helped you see that there are some changes you want to keep. "I don't ever want to go back to that feeling of futility." "I don't ever want to go back to fighting God at every step."

So what can you put in place that will help?

Implementation intentions.[1]

I know. It doesn't sound very spiritual. But sometimes the most spiritual step we can take is the most practical.

Here's a little background.

Habits are patterns of behavior with three parts: a cue, a reward, and a routine. When there is a cue (stress) we perform the routine (eat chocolate) to experience the reward (a kick). When there is a cue (angry caller) we perform the routine

[1] http://en.wikipedia.org/wiki/Implementation_intention

(hang up the phone) to experience the reward (quiet). When there is a cue (angry comment from a child) we perform the routine (yell "shut up") to experience the reward (relief of stress).

As illustrated by the last example, sometimes our habits provide short-lived or destructive rewards. Extensive research says that we can create instant habits by identifying a cue and then identifying a behavior, a routine, that we will perform. It can be a better routine.

The key is that we phrase these implementation intentions as specifically as possible, using the form "IF this situation happens, THEN this is what I will do."

For example: "IF I am reaching to set my alarm clock, THEN I will say "Thanks, God, we made it."

I know. It feels like we should say "When" rather than "If." But it doesn't work that way.

So what if we apply this research to our life following Jesus? What if we say, "I want to live more like Jesus calls me to live"?

Let me offer 33 practical commitments that might help you:

1. If I see an email from *that* person, then I will ask God for wisdom before I open the email.

2. If it is morning and I'm just looking at my computer, then I will spend ten minutes every morning before I check my email sitting in that rocking chair and talking with God about what I'm worried about.

3. If I am feeling stressed and am reaching for a piece of chocolate, then I will say "God, in the same way that

this chocolate will satisfy a craving, would you satisfy my craving for peace?"

4. If I feel attacked for doing what God wants, then I will respond like David who asked God to rescue him from evildoers.

5. If I wake up without a headache, then I will say "Thank you, God."

6. If I get a text from my child, then I will say, "Thank you, God, for this child."

7. If it is Monday morning, then I will read Psalm 19 and say the end as a prayer.

8. If a person's name comes to mind in an unexpected way, then I will ask God how I can help that person.

9. If it is the first day of the month, then I will spend one hour asking God to help me review the previous month looking for evidences of his work.

10. If I wake in the middle of the night and am afraid, then I will call out the name of Jesus.

11. If someone says, "Will you forgive me", then I will say, "I forgive you."

12. If someone says, "Thank you," I will say, "You're welcome."

13. If my child says, "Tell me about God", then I will.

14. If God says my name, then I will say, "Here I am."

15. I will change the caller ID in my phone for Person X to "Person X, loved by God" (I know. It's not IF...THEN. But it's a good idea.)

16. If I see my spouse carrying a heavy load, then I will say, "How can I help?"

17. If someone says, "How was your week?", then I will say, "I've been learning and growing. What about you?"

18. If I can turn off the background noise, then I will choose silence.

19. If I can give time to change the world or to watch TV, then I will give time to change the world.

20. If I am feeling confused about whether a business decision is about my kingdom or God's, then I will stop everything and ask God for wisdom.

21. If I haven't written "talk with God" on my schedule, then I will schedule a fifteen minute conversation with God for each of the next three days.

22. If I believe even a little bit that God can work, then I will ask him to work.

23. If I get a paycheck, then I will give ten percent of it to God.

24. If a conversation turns to gossip, then I will walk out of the conversation.

25. If I am sitting in church and remember that I made someone mad, then I will go make it right.

26. If I am about to attack someone verbally for their disobedience, then I will first look at my own disobedience.

27. If I promised to be home at 5:00 and it is 5:00, then I

will tell God that I lied, and I will go home.

28. If I see I am procrastinating on completing a promised task, then I will ask God if I'm being a perfectionist.

29. If I am afraid of the future, then I will cry out to God.

30. If I am unwilling to forgive someone, then I will ask God "why can't I?"

31. If I don't want to go to church, then I will find a follower of Jesus to have a conversation with.

32. If I am having an emotional affair, then I will stop right now.

33. If I am outside and it is night, then I will look at the sky and say, "The heavens declare the Glory of God."

ABOUT THE AUTHOR

Jon Swanson helps people understand following God.

For thirty years, he has regularly taught about Jesus and the Bible in small groups, Sunday School classes, and since 2009, at 300wordsaday.com. He brings his background in communication and higher education to his study and teaching, looking for the stories and voices of the people in the Bible.

Jon and Nancy were engaged after a walk to the family cemetery and were married in 1983, during the spring break of his first year of doctoral studies. Nancy has worked in higher education and non-profits and her garden. She helps good things grow well. They have three children: Andrew, who married Allie, Kathryn (deceased) and Hope, who married Dan.

Since 2016, he has been a chaplain and consultant and mentor. Before that he was an associate pastor, most recently serving as executive pastor at Grabill Missionary Church. Before that, he worked in higher education as a faculty member and administrator.

Jon holds a BA from Wheaton College, a MA from Northern Illinois University, and a PhD from The University of Texas at Austin, all in communication studies.

He is ordained in the Missionary Church.

He has written four other books.

A Great Work: A Conversation With Nehemiah For People (Who Want To Be) Doing Great Works.

Anticipation. An Advent Reader.

Learning a New Routine. Reading the Sermon on the Mount a Little Bit at a Time.

Saint John of the Mall. Reflections for the Advent Season.

And as more books are published, you can learn about them at ANewRoutine.com.

And, if you found this book helpful, before you go, would you be willing to recommend it for others?

Thanks for spending this time together.

Connect with Jon online:

Twitter: http://www.twitter.com/jnswanson

Facebook: http://www.facebook.com/jnswanson

Blog: http://300wordsaday.com

APPENDIX: COFFEE FOR LENT: A LENTEN MEMOIR.

I'm a protestant. An evangelical protestant. I didn't grow up with Lent. My friend Chris did grow up with Lent. He lived across the street and down a couple houses. He always gave up watermelon for Lent. It was perfect. Though he loved watermelon, winter watermelon hadn't been invented back then. I think he gave up licorice, too.

As I got older, I began to explore the idea of spiritual disciplines, of learning about discipline. For reasons that I don't remember, in 1989, I decided to take Lent seriously, to give up something that mattered.

I can't remember why. In fact, it wasn't until I start thinking about writing this essay, until I started telling you why a protestant, evangelical, college professor cares about Lent, that I understood how much I gave up that year.

I thought I was giving up coffee. I ended up giving up my heart. And, eventually, finding Hope.

You can stop reading now, if you want. This is going to get worse before it gets better. Before we are done, someone is going die.

But I suppose that's what Lent is about. It's about dying, in particular to self. It's about finding out what it means to willingly give up something that matters.

In that, I think, Lent has more to do with Philippians than with fasting.

Sorry. We're going to get biblical here as well. You can run now. Bible and death. And Lent.

But I'm glad you are still here.

How I gave up coffee

In 1989, I was a college professor. I taught communication. Every Thursday afternoon, several of us had a coffee break in the staff lounge at the end of my hallway.

Those breaks were just one of the times I drank coffee. Because the pot was close, because the coffee was free, I drank eight or ten mugs of caffeinated coffee in a day. Every weekday. I got headaches on Saturday. It took awhile to figure out why.

In 1989, in my fifth year at a college that didn't make much of Lent, that didn't even know when it was, I gave up coffee. I decided that year that I needed to pick something that mattered, something habitual. Coffee was perfect.

What I gave up was everything but one cup of coffee a day. I wasn't going to be a legalist, an extremist. But I wanted to give up something that would make me think every time I would reach for a mug.

That's what Lent is about, by the way. It's a forty-day season of fasting, extending from Ash Wednesday to Good Friday.

You are thinking about the calendar. You know there are more than forty days in there. And you are right. It's forty days of fasting in a forty-eight day span. You keep Sabbath, even from fasting. Because we need rest. We need to know that the value is not in giving up. It's in understanding that there is a good greater than the good things we give up.

I gave up coffee. I knew that there would be a challenge, both in the habit of drinking and the energy. All but one cup a day. I believed that I would be more likely to succeed if I allowed myself to appreciate one cup, to treasure it. And then realized that it was the end of the most important time of my doctoral research.

The long story of my doctoral studies is not for here. The classroom part starts in September, 1982, in Austin, Texas. In 1985, finished with the classroom part and starting on the dissertation writing part, Nancy and I moved to Fort Wayne (Indiana), to Fort Wayne Bible College. I taught full-time and spent lots of time trying to study, trying to research, trying to write. By 1989, I had wrestled through procrastination and confusion and was finishing writing the argument. I was counting down to deadline. I would defend my dissertation on Good Friday, at the end of that season of Lent.

And I was going to be ready, caffeine headaches or not.

A baby on the way
But there is another thread to this story, happening inside Nancy.

Andrew was born February 25, 1987. And we discovered before Christmas 1988, that Nancy was expecting again. We decided to tell my family in a cute way. We took a couple verses from Psalm 139, wrote them on paper, put them inside baby food jars.

For you created my inmost being;
you knit me together in my mother's womb.
I praise you because
I am fearfully and wonderfully made;
your works are wonderful,
I know that full well.
My frame was not hidden from you
when I was made in the secret place.
When I was woven together
in the depths of the earth,
your eyes saw my unformed body.
All the days ordained for me
were written in your book
before one of them came to be.

Psalm 139:13-16

My family opened their jars. And looked at us. It was too subtle. We had to explain. There was another baby coming.

Sometime that winter, in the usual tests that are done for babies, there came a question. "It could be nothing. It could be this or that. You should have an amniocentesis."

It included an ultrasound. We saw the baby.

And so, on Wednesday morning, March 22, 1989, we sat

with the geneticist and heard that our baby girl had Trisomy 18. She might live until birth, though the chances were one in two. If she lived a long time, she might make it to her first birthday.

That afternoon, we drove from Indiana to Illinois. On Thursday we flew to Texas. On Friday I defended my dissertation. On Sunday I drank coffee. And we flew back to Illinois. And we thought about Easter and the joy. In that one week I learned that I would be a doctor, and we learned that we would lose a daughter.

Waiting through pregnancy is like Lent. It is discomfort and disruption which we endure because there is great delight at the end.

Katherine Anne Swanson was born on July 28, 1989. She lived for five weeks. She died on Friday, September 1, 1989.

On Saturday, we buried her body.

Sabbath as completion of God's work

With every burial we understand a bit of the disciples' sense of loss between Jesus' death and resurrection. Good Friday, great pain. Sunday, great delight. Saturday. Great ache. Great hollowness. Creation aches. On that Sabbath between death and resurrection of Jesus, there was no rest or restoration. It couldn't have been a Sabbath for the disciples.

Or was it?

Mark Buchanan writes in *The Rest of God* about the two versions of the command to remember the Sabbath. When Exodus lists the commandments, the people are told to keep the Sabbath holy because on that day God rested. Forty years later, when Moses is teaching the people one last time in Deuteronomy, he says to keep the Sabbath holy because God rescued them from their Egyptian task masters. God rested, God gave rest.[2]

On this Sabbath, after the most traumatic work possible, after dying for the lost creation, Jesus was dead. But in Jesus' words "It is finished", there is hope. Something is done. And the Sabbath was to remember the deliverance. God bringing Israel out of Egypt. With a mighty hand and outstretched arm. No one living on that day understood how much Jesus had done, knew that restoration and reconciliation were on their way.

On the morning of Kate's burial, our small house was busy. The living room and kitchen and yard were full of people. Both sides of family, some seeing each other for the first time since our wedding. Seven years of catching up, tempered by the context. I stood in our small upstairs bedroom. I cried. And I cried out.

I couldn't yell. Too many people. But I yelled nonetheless. "I do not understand." I told God. "I know you are God, but I do not understand."

I may not have the words right. It's been two decades and more. But I see out the second floor window to the stone

[2] Mark Buchanan. *The Rest of God.* Nashville: W Publishing Group, 2006. Chapter 6 explains the two views of Sabbath.

driveway. I feel the slanty ceiling of our bedroom compressing the thoughts, pointing them up. I remember that for the first time in my life I wasn't worrying about the words. I wasn't considering shades of meaning. Words dragged across the raw edges of my soul. My chest was collapsing. My left arm ached with emptiness where it had held our daughter as she stopped breathing.

And then it was time to go. To ride in the first car in the informal procession. To look out the window at the people who stopped looking back. To stop by the big tree and walk to the small hole and see the tiny box on the platform.

A baby casket is a little thing.

We sat there, Nancy and I. I don't remember people around. I don't remember what my colleague Carl said. I don't remember leaving. But I remember the sun and the box and the pile of dirt behind.

And I remember this:

In the middle of whatever else happened. I felt something inside. You know that feeling we describe as butterflies in your stomach, that sense of anxiety before a major event? The sense you have before you stand to speak? Take the opposite of that. Not a deadness, not at all. But a moving peace like the moving fear.

And that peace stayed for the day, through the conversations, through the meal.

Peace that makes no sense.

God gives peace at moments that make no sense.

At times when by every right everything emotionally should be cascading in, there can be peace. Not a denial, but an acknowledgment that yes, indeed, there is cancer, but God has a clue. Not a denial but an acknowledgment that yes, that casket holds the body of an infant daughter, but God is present.

Ah, but the peace doesn't come because suddenly everything makes sense: "If I get cancer, then other people will understand that life is important and so my life, however short, will accomplish something."

That kind of explaining would allow us to arrive at peace as some rationalization of suffering. And I'm not sure that's what Paul means when he writes,

"Do not be anxious about anything, but in everything, by prayer and petition, with thanksgiving, present your requests to God. And the peace of God, which transcends all understanding, will guard your hearts and your minds in Christ Jesus." (Philippians 4:6-7)

I know. We want a recipe. We want to know that we will understand why things are the way they are. And in these two sentences there is no promise of understanding. There is no promise that things will work out fine.

Instead, Paul says that our hearts and our minds, those things that churn and process and spin and struggle in the middle of pain and chaos and ambiguity and inadequacy, will be guarded.

I suppose that part of the guarding comes from inviting someone else into the discussion. Knowing that someone who is capable of acting on our behalf is aware of the problem gives peace. But sometimes, nonsensical peace, incomprehensible peace, is an evidence of God, offered to rational minds in danger of spinning out of control.

Like mine.

ACKNOWLEDGMENTS

In 2009, we asked a group of friends to meet for six weeks on Saturday nights for soup and study. We ate soup. And then we talked about prayer and solitude and other spiritual practices. It was Lent, though we never talked about it. That six weeks lasted for nearly eight years. We work out what it means to follow Jesus every week. I am grateful to Ken, Gayle, Jaala, Paul, Lisa, Dick, Jill, Mark, Linda, Kyle, John, Deb, Kirk, Joy, and Nancy.

The readers of 300wordsaday.com make me think, encourage me, challenge me, and help me more than they know. I cannot list them by name. But I am grateful to them.

Andrew and Allie and Hope and Dan have formed me as much as I have formed them. They have taught me about being a dad and about having a heavenly dad.

Nancy and I go walking almost every day. Those conversations for the past decade show us both that following Jesus is about discipline and relationship. And delight.

And I do not blame God for my bad writing or inept understandings. But I am grateful that He invites me to keep trying to understand and express our relationship.